Everything Flows

A Compilation of Art, Photos, and Poetry

From my heart to yours.

Thank you for taking the time to read my poetry. I have wanted to publish this project for so long and I am ecstatic to finally share this with you. May you perceive these words by your own context. For now, it's yours.

With lots of love,
Nichole

L.O.V.E

Like
Overflowing
Vibes
Elating

Free

Keep faking the front.
It won't take long, no
Real ones find the mask.
Jazzy said, "No love lost"
Bell was the fool but never the cost

Fly

I summon me to myself
Ain't no trying to be "she"
In this life of stranger, friend, or foe
No one loves me more than me.
Box cutter to the pressure

-I'm free

The Message

We are not obligated to all the answers

Fall away from the mundane-lane

Down may be your bets

But in time life has a way to repay

We are going to trip and fall sometimes

Get back to why you began

Up is where it was worth it all, to fall,

and fight again

Yes

"No", can not be the answer!

One more death is considered a

tragedy!

Needs of humanity, seize!

Another law must be enforced.

Fight universally for compassion

to be endorsed.

Courage

Make It Work

I've landed on a plateau
Hard to escape after this long.
The fever of failure grows
Has me sick of myself and my wrongs

I thought to myself
Like a hero in the night.
You never give up on self
For with resilience, I know, comes a
fight

My dreams made me Hulk up.
A life worth living is uphill
So, find the mountains -I thought

Then something whispered inside my will

"Remember, life is what you make it.
Shape those mountains.
Activate the crust of opportunity.
Rise one inch at a time from the pit, from
within"

And I know at the top will be home.
Don't be afraid of steep steps.
For something far worse than falling is a
plateau.
Take a leap of depth, the Universe got
your bets

Crossroads

Far, far from being faultless or perfect
But confidence I salute and elect
All my blunder and ridges
I try to craft bridges
Desperately reaching to be on track

Seeking the better me

Sacrificing the comfort of gleam
Of being spotlessly seen
Considering that truth goes a long way
I come alive in a real way -every time
I come clean

And I create more room for building the
real and fulfilled me

Soul

Spirit Experience

Everyday is sacred
I call to the Heavens, "Deliver me
strength"
My flesh does not have what it takes
to render myself
My soul calls to the Heavens,
"Salvage me!"
I surrender
The key to my flesh
And my destiny

Destined to Believe

After four years, I've don't a lot, yet…
I feel, I've done nothing at all
But how? I am still here, stacked
Packed to get to the top
I don't flip flop, no
My focused flow
Can't, won't stop
Dreaming
A lil dream
To love yourself
Yes, is to believe
And to live your best life
So yes, try, for trying is
Most definitely, believing

Breathe

Centered (Ode)

Today my hopelessness realized
Everything controlled is within.
The world can be a chaotic demise
But I can occupy peace times ten.

It can be the thunderstorm now
But it never stops the rainbow from
stepping in.
Oh, in the midst of a storm
It can feel like the sun has somehow
Abandoned you -weeping within
But, the truth is, light resides inside your
form

This peace I carry inside
Feels like God sent.
Like the nectar of gratitude on a dreary
ride
I'm alive and my wings are merely wet.

Now, I know why breathing deep needs
to seep
It's life, it's important
It hooks your life from the core, and
centers you intact.
The storm may have ransacked my path
and made flight hard to keep.
But, that favorably strengthened my
center into purpose, reassuring me.
Providing the only light where I'm at.

And with this I need nothing more
When I'm the light waiting at Sun's
door.

One Way

One way, less traveled
Dance, stumble, fly, idle
Battles by the mile

Tripped from glancing back, made it the
dance
But, in this life sometimes, there is only
one chance
Leave your mark -stop glancing back

Only lessons are reminiscent
To better mold the present
Only one way, that is forward, be
persistent

On the trail or through rough terrain
Clear skies or rain
Remember the way

OBJECTS
CLOSE

Fortitude

Ever Knowing

Discernment, the sageness of maturity
The value of patience
And, the judgement on when to set my
truth free

Discernment is the insight of certainty and
common sense
The humbleness of validity
And, knowing all that I possess, doesn't
have to hatch or be pushed off the fence

My two cents doesn't need to power over
mid-city
For what value is that?

Discernment means to rest and when the
direction in que is set
I speak more valid and witty

Not just when I want to say something,
driving from the back
But when the message is destined to leak
Every facet on track

Discernment, the deeper process of power
and release.
And, even when I'm silent – I know
ever knowing peace

Shhhhhh

Calculate your steps but flow
like water